Dearest T[illegible]

My al[illegible] or of

public profile.

You represented a father figure

to me, and those of my generation.

Thank you for your contribution &

carrying this mantle.

I hope you enjoy this book.

With love to you & your

family.

[illegible]

Humans don't just search the archive; we are the archive.

EINZ

Book Cover by O. Hayat | Illustrations by DALL·E 2 | Ed. JED

Print ISBN: 978-3-00-076930-6 | Ebook ISBN: 978-3-00-076929-0

First Edition

PREFACE

I wrote this for my children. When my father died last year, I wished I had something of his essence to keep and explore. He was an African man of the 1950s, so I never expected an open book; his generation is strong but emotionally quiet.

Herein, we will explore my favourite subjects in short form through narrative and debate. The ideas were well-researched; nevertheless, this is not an academic text; it is the first volume of a provocative series. Beyond the personal, this is intended to bring philosophical subjects to the public through the debate of current affairs.

Divergent, abstract thinking should be for all, not some. It is incumbent on us, as humans, to know what we believe and why. We love, we think, and we seek.

Above all, we are sovereign.

CONTENTS

EINZ

Vol. I

CHAPTER I

GOD & SCIENCE

In truth, the sun might well be setting on orthodox religion. Won't we miss the beautiful ancient stories told by our grandparents, and what of the enduring life lessons we owe to scripture? Where is God to you? If you don't believe, ask yourself the best case you could muster in defence of God's existence. Convictions aside, do you sense a presence in your moments of growth, love, or even in suffering? I do. Above all, God is most evident in the moment I decide to trust.

From survival to art to the answers we seek today, our consciousness was invited to unfold over millennia. But invited by what? That pull civilised us to the moment we upped and bailed, The Age of Reason. Those newfound threads convinced us that enlightenment was ours and ours alone. However, long before we could debate this existence, before history itself, our story began with a palaeolithic yearning for beauty; they engraved, they buried, and they prayed. This was a call to transcendence, not to science. And nothing has changed.

In any event, the wolf is at the door. The West perceives religion with ever-diminishing credibility and relevance. Ultimately, the debate should be with God, not the broker. Perpetually, religion finds its dated texts in some kind of PR hash-up. Christianity seems most vulnerable to this, ceding the ground of its principles to the latest zeitgeist. But the returns on political correctness evaporate from one moment to the next. And for all their apologising, redacting and revising, they still find themselves persona non grata.

Holding court are the more outspoken atheist scientists, from Dawkins to Hitchens; God rest his soul. They have trifled with the weakest rung of this debate. Instead of defending science with honour by directly addressing the God question, the most relevant and challenging test of critical reasoning, rather, they cut loose and serve us with a tedious assault on religion. Recounting the brutal horrors of religious texts and laying the burden of human conflict at the door of religion is as washed-up as it gets. In burying the God discussion in shame and deferring to religion, atheists expected this age-old debate would never have its day. This chapter will show how this gridlock has short-changed us all.

The very act of skirting the God question is quite revealing; atheism's anxiety around God confirms to all and sundry that herein lies a formidable concept - one to be reckoned with. Whether you bat offence or defence on this one, the case must be levelled at God because if the focus is upon religious prescription and not the love of God, then something has gone deeply awry. God is not bound by religion. And the love of God is not some hollow team sport. We, however, will meet this debate at its point of puncture, balancing the evidence for God whilst assessing science's authority as it wagers its coup d'état.

Curiously, atheists and die-hard believers don't just push my buttons; they push all the same damn buttons. Specifically, the ignorance of mainstream religious believers just persists. We've all watched one zealot or another confronted with an unexpected yet credible question from the atheist's opposing position. You stand there, swirling your glass, as they discretely size up the damage. It already feels like weeks of elusive gazing for you, but not for them; adrenals jacked, frisking scripture's position, leaving just enough time to rephrase and pass it all off as organic, and they bid their response. You brace yourself for a long-winded song and dance. And if they're feeling especially iffy, they'll spam you and anyone listening with chapter and verse citations. Alternatively, they'll just throw in the sponge and chalk it all to 'The mystery of God.' Perfect.

Science can be equally sketchy. Despite an avid interest in philosophy and the arts, physics was my first love. In an unpredictable world of infinite possibilities, the sense of clarity and security borne of the laws of classical physics was, and in part remains, quite comforting. Though heartbreak wasn't far behind once I realised the rulebook would not universally apply to all that we have come to know, let alone to that which we are yet to discover. Indeed, those laws require a sizable disclaimer.

Many, if not all of us have encountered miracles, and whilst I'm inclined to accept the authenticity of a miraculous event when I hear of it, I also acknowledge that to some cynics, such stories are not so easily digested. Moreover, to those whose soul is so dimly lit, the very act of sharing a miraculous story, never mind its bewildering content, is settled as trite. So, in this chapter, I'll save the long-form personal narrative and instead share pieces of me as we go. But before we cut to the debate, let's consider where we are. The following is a selection of unanswered or underexplored phenomena for which science and the religious community should be held accountable. I'm not suggesting that either side should understand the mechanics of our entire reality; rather, they might both consider less of the smug get-up since we know we're all equally lost on the questions of existence.

Modern science's hard rejection of the metaphysical is reminiscent of the Ancient Greek's fear of the number zero. This resistance, rallied by Pythagoras, was so effective that by the Socratic era, it was convention. Eastern cultures embraced zero, allowing Arabs and Indians a significant advance in mathematics during this period. In contrast, Aristotle was instrumental in banning the use of the number zero in discourse and markets; this rippled through the West for 1500 years, a wanton suppression of the wonders of math. Tolerance for zero recovered incrementally until its renaissance in the 17th century.

One moment, we're denying the significance of zero, and the next, we're banding about the concept of infinity. When quantifying the value and meaning of zero or infinity, we're taken to the edge of our conceptual limits. One might see birth in zero: a child, an idea, or even the Universe's beginning. Infinity represents immortality, perhaps of consciousness, math, or even the virtues which underwrite math. Is there even any difference between these numbers or concepts? Their philosophical significance is undeniable yet is deliberately muted. Why that? Regardless, the wonder of zero endures; just how is it that zero becomes one? I can get behind other mathematical sequences. However, zero to one, non-existence to existence, this knocks me clean. German-American tech entrepreneur Peter Thiel captures the beauty of this step in his book *Zero to One*, "The act of creation is singular, as is the moment of creation..."

For centuries, math has provided shelter for atheists, insulating them from the ambiguity of life. Of course, there's no doubting the great comfort provided by that which structures science and reason. However, the irony here is that math is spirituality. The beauty of math in its order, kindred in perfect unity with nature's wild infinite, compels us to question how this balance comes to be within the Universe - and indeed ourselves. Math demands our integrity. In violation of truth or faith, our equations will not balance. Rising to a mathematical challenge requires dedication, faith if you will, and the sense of reward is transcendent, if only for a moment. Math and the Universe begin with the question of zero to one, a step that has proven impossible to recreate in the life sciences. Still, in nature, we exist, so it happened and continues to happen. The impossible manifests with or without our permission.

Empiricism's blind spots are strewn across academia. However, some are rather profound in the context of science and the metaphysical and thus deserve our attention. Quantum physics presents us with the phenomena of wave-particle duality; experiments have illustrated that an apparently inanimate particle behaves differently in the presence of an observer or particle detector. Since humans and objects are constituted of particles, does this then mean we might also be waves, not just here or there, but perhaps everywhere? The Copenhagen Interpretation, Pilot-Wave Theory, Many Worlds and others offer some explanations for this wonder; nevertheless, the implications here are not to be understated. I'm left questioning if any part of reality exists independent of observation, or is the Universe merely white noise until the point of recognition? At the very least, reality is altered, if not determined, by observation. Quantum physics is exposing the vulnerabilities of science's most fundamental assumptions. Seriously, why isn't this news?

Absolute objectivity is a pipedream; this has held true long after British mathematician Bertrand Russell laid it clear. Experimental rigour is a game of dress-up since we're still in and of the soup we wish to study. And the extent of our misfires, how could we possibly know? Moreover, how could we conceive an experiment that proves the existence of God? Douglas Adams explores this dilemma in his *Hitchhiker's Guide to the Galaxy*. Adams seems amused by our approach to the puzzle of existence that its answer might already be in our possession if only we knew which question to ask. Despair not, though, double-hatting as lab-coat and lab-rat hasn't blown all the fun. We've tremendously improved life here on Earth, and science will undoubtedly continue to cater to our practical needs. But expecting science to plate up anything more fundamental or metaphysical may be as wishful as its hold on objectivity.

Would you agree that it's high time physics took the floor on its unfinished business and brought us on in? After all, a problem shared... So, how do entangled particles separated by vast distances, potentially lightyears apart, communicate with one another at all, let alone faster than the speed of light? And if we accept that since the Big Bang, the Universe has been simultaneously cooling, expanding, indeed accelerating, all whilst rejecting gravity's charms, then at least loop us in on the secret. The truth is, we know next to nothing about the dark energy source propelling this inflation. NASA states that dark energy constitutes 68% of the Universe; however, its properties remain invisible because it interacts with nothing bar gravity, and its detection is all the more dispiriting. In 1929, astronomer Edwin Hubble observed evidence of its expansion. Since then, the Universe has offered up scraps for our pining; just for the squeeze, she invites us to run our audits on her properties, only to watch us watch her whisper sweet nothings lightyears after the fact.

To be clear, this force which occupies much of the Universe is not only indestructible and thus far unknowable; it travels at twice the speed of light whilst hauling the entire Universe.

This will eventually spread us too far and too cold even to exist, let alone pick up any TikToks from the past. And for those who don't spook easy, resolve this; dark energy chases its expanse without losing or gaining a single unit of anything, infinite energy. Isn't it curious that when its natural laws come up short, science is out to lunch? And yet, if ever there were an element so omnipotent and immortal, empirically unprovable yet entirely plausible, that it could only be dark energy, right? *Schade.* Science is more than willing to cough up a hall pass for dear dark energy's dissent whilst extending no such grace for any other concept or philosophy. At the height of this hypocrisy is the difference between the verifiable properties of dark energy and God. None.

And then there's Artificial Intelligence (AI). We're all super excited about the future of AI while simultaneously worried about the system gaining consciousness or singularity. Consciousness? That's a hard no. Singularity? Absolutely. I should note that I'm more concerned about AI being used by humans to nefarious ends. Global powers interested in destabilising Western civilisation might ink their plans sooner than AI's divergence. AI is indeed impressive, but the natural brain isn't merely defined, valued, or, indeed, limited by its computational processing power. Still, we'll concede; when scored today by the speed and accuracy of its linear thinking, then fine, we've hit the skids. AI's potential is remarkable, particularly as it broadens its range of convertible data and aligns its path with holographic data storage innovations. AI researcher Brian Roemmele is an inspiring speaker on creating a localised personal AI that would track the data we're exposed to throughout our lifetime. It would advise and partner with us, ultimately allowing us to operate at untold levels of efficiency. That's kind of cool, and it's just one avenue. AI will step into another dimension once it ties the knot with quantum systems. Farewell to the binds of serial and parallel computing, quantum is about to pimp this ride, no more coy reserve, cart before the horse; the liberation of AI spells a new age for genetic research, pharma, space and those are just the headline industries.

Notwithstanding the hype, there is a line, the width of the Universe, dividing the imitation of understanding staged by synthetic intelligence and authentic understanding characteristic only of sentient beings. The difference here is consequential. Only we are genuinely moved by beauty and traumatised by tragedy; life is no spectator sport. Intense emotions elicit a holistic reaction; the intellectual response is just a slice of the action. What about the physiological, the chills, the butterflies? And no, I do not believe an AI will ever sense physical experience as we do.

The senses uniquely indulge us with rich, potent, nebulous feelings which arouse, inform, and invigorate the next iteration of our development. Even attempting to architect an experience close to this resolution would demand an invention capable of processing a spectrum of physical and mental stimuli, saturating fields of imagination akin to ours, scrutinising its own perception, and employing logic when it pleases, only to leave it in the dust for something so much more. Consciousness. A holistic re-creation of the human experience is well above the smarts of any engineer. Question: Larry Page, how do you celebrate AI's intelligence in the absence of its capacity to understand? Moreover, how do you imagine a digital God without consciousness? Such experiences AI could only dream of paraphrasing. If only it could dream. Humans don't just search the archive; we are the archive.

Never have I felt intimidated by AI. I may fail to flip an actuarial model on demand, but that's more likely an indication of our incomplete understanding of brain ops. Consider the savants who compose a masterpiece or perform instant calculations of 8–100-digit numbers, often without studying music or math. We know the brain buries AI; we just don't know how. Digitising millimetres of human brain architecture or all the wily smarts of the larval fruit fly has sunk oceans. Never mind that; call me once we've created a single living biological cell, and *no*, a synthetic cell comprised of repurposed DNA, RNA, proteins, and other wonders courtesy of Mother Nature's apron strings will not qualify. Quite the anti-climax, right? A woeful crack at zero to one.

If you're partial to a spot of bioengineering, you might appreciate the advances made during the last decade, which has seen stem cell derivates used to develop brain organoids in-vitro, yum. By rejigging the soup's nourishing ingredients, researchers have grown promising organoids that at least get to celebrate one or two birthdays. Better still, adding a smidge of vascular cultures creates a more self-sustaining medley. This might be exciting for disease research, but Mary Shelley wants a word.

Turns out 'Creator' is more than just a stage name. Who, in a line-up of NEST, IBM, Blue Brain Project, DARPA, Human Brain Project or wherever else, could engineer a holistic simulation which could bid its way through the functional standard as set by the human brain? Let's itemise: sensing, selecting, intellectual/emotional interpreting, editing, encoding, executing, communicating verbally/behaviourally, and coordinating physical action, all whilst simultaneously localising energetic expenditure and attention to optimise productivity. And still, there are the brain's unconscious homeostatic chores and neural upgrades; these alone clock up a processing demand of 11 million bits of sensory data per heartbeat. That's some rap sheet, and here, we're only assuming a static state. Imagine if we included the impact of a dynamic state rendered by external stressors, ill health, or the fanciful pursuits of consciousness.

Then there's time. The remarkable precision with which the brain unconsciously tracks the passage of time through its dual systems of the 24-hour circadian clock and the record of our life story. The latter sees it overlay our real-time sensory feed with timestamps with a pattern that is still yet to be fully understood. Neurons fire to record episodic chapters of content rather than just the mundane passage of time, and the reel is flawless. When kept in balance, this quaint library of events synchronises perfectly with our nearest observatory, corresponding seamlessly to the beat of the Universe.

One week ago, the memory of my late father brought me to my knees. In a conscious effort to move towards the pain, I opened the WhatsApp messages I had archived following his funeral. Until last week, I hadn't found the strength to read them. As I opened the file, I realised that August 24th 2022, was the last time he tried to call me but could not reach me, and precisely one year later, almost to the hour, without a reason, I broke down uncontrollably. That clock is something else. But that's not all. We can manipulate time; as Einstein's special relativity intimates, the brain can slow down the sense of time on demand in surrender to an experience of awe or watching the phone expectantly, not quite as fun. Speeding up time is simple; we pack our schedule.

And if you're expecting AI to surpass the brain's data warehousing capacities, you might sell us short. So far, the brain has a memory conservatively estimated at 1 to 2.5 petabytes. For context, the European Space Agency is conducting an ongoing discovery mission to produce the Milky Way's most extensive and precise 3D map. Launched in December 2013, Spacecraft Gaia is expected to catalogue the properties of two billion objects, the data for which will reach or exceed one petabyte. Moreover, in order to fuel its 100bn processors (neurons) or trillions of synapses, the brain consumes the energy equivalent to a good camping torch, 20 watts. In 2013, K, Japan's supercomputer, debuted its brain simulator, mimicking 1 second of real-time brain activity took 40 minutes for K. This technology runs on a modest 12 megawatts, enough to power 12,000 suburban homes. What lies here is much more than a story of efficiencies. If 20 watts is accurate, how do we balance the thermodynamics? Should we smile politely at an equation flanked either side by the power of a light bulb and a data centre? And if 20 watts is a gross underestimation, then from what or where does the brain supplement this colossal deficit? Isn't this fascinating, yet we are more interested in the wannabe technology over the real deal? Go figure. None of this diminishes AI's potential impact on the world, but when this knock-off is marked against the enigma of consciousness, that's enough to make Guangzhou blush.

We could broaden our engineering lens, leaving more space to comprehend existence. But who knows, if the secret to the meaning of life has been hidden in plain sight, waiting for quantum to be just a little less Jenga and finally take charge of parsing every byte of data known to Man to end this debate, then Hail Mary; perhaps a piece of tech will indeed beat us to it. Still, before we cut the cards on that prospect, dial back to the archive; soft copy data became a useable technology in the early 1970s, developing into the advanced storage cloud solutions of the present day. That's a lot of data, a nourishing environment for AI's burgeoning knowledge base. However, there is one data source that could give the post-WW records a run for its content.

Our richest natural intelligence resource is the wealth of ancestral information encoded into our genes. Prof. Oded Rechavi, a leading expert in transgenerational biology, has dedicated his lab research to exploring the epigenetics of memory. Concentrating on the transfer, expression, and retention of physiological and behavioural changes, Prof.

Rechavi and his team have proved that memories are heritable over multiple generations, as demonstrated by the research conducted on C. elegans. Firstly, the worms were exposed to an odour followed by starvation conditions. Experiments showed that in defence, subjects synthesised protective sRNA molecules; these were transmitted to future generations, reinforcing the natural longevity of the descendants. But curiously, the first few future generations also expressed an aversion to the odour from the initial experiment. However, the descendants had not been exposed to the smell; therefore, this knowledge was indeed inherited.

We needn't wait another X decades only to confirm the results produced by Prof. Rechavi's team bear resonance with our species. We know now that the potency of the memory's expression across future generations is determined by the levels of environmental stress endured at the moment of encoding; therefore, the higher the stress levels, the more resilient the memory. So, if data derived from the trials of previous civilisations rests within our present-day DNA, well, what's it worth? Two hundred millennia of evolutionary arsenal coded into the 2023 human genome, and this, dear AI, is wisdom inaccessible on the cloud.

Imagining the capabilities of AI superintelligence (ASI), yes, the one that gains singularity; ultimately, we're still talking about an advanced multi-layer processor operating at quantum speeds. However, speed isn't all that helpful in a system trapped by reason, deprived of true wisdom. Much like a few academics I know, AI is at grave risk of accepting its computational conclusions wholesale. Without a higher abstract counsel to temper its logical excesses, the path to singularity is linear. Consciousness is the essence of the human being, the ultimate decider, philosopher, dreamer, lover, an algorithm so pure, so divine, steeped in the best of you. This one, neuroscientists cannot even find, let alone copy.

Science has contributed immeasurably to humanity, improving fertility, longevity, education, defence, interconnectivity, monetary systems and ultimately, freedom. As Harvard Prof. Steven Pinker's *Enlightenment Now* details, we have elevated economic conditions to levels which facilitate the pursuit of enlightenment. Science and spirituality go hand in hand.

God enduringly offers us an indispensable tool for spiritual survival, rescuing the individual at the countless critical times when science proves - yet for which it pays no apology - its pitiful impotence. When devastated by grief, heartbreak, bankruptcy or one of the infinite paths to tragedy, it is in these intractable moments the value of rationality is exposed, no more than a common prop in our dystopia. Wouldn't life be so peachy if we could balance our soul with a healthy diet/ exercise regimen and remind ourselves daily that there is no God? Much better.

Something tells me that the truth of our existence could remain unknown and unproven indefinitely. Or that may change when we are ready.

Debate

Design of Matter

St Anselm's 11th-century ontological position echoes throughout the millennia that follow, and for good reason. It's challenging to refute the core idea underpinning this deism. Last I checked, no one's topped the concept of God. And then there's the sheer magnificence of nature and its captivating order, expressed in its beauty, power, and governance bestowed by its natural laws. The complex and improbable conditions which gave rise to the cosmos and eukaryogenesis are a marvel. Moreover, the hierarchies that have emerged and evolved within, between and across the species. None of this rings unintentional.

Beauty is infinite, so I'll stop at the one that grips me: the perilous electrochemical dance that occurs as we metabolise glucose into energy and CO2. Credit to British biochemist and 20th-century Nobel prize winner Peter Mitchell, who blended the sciences to reveal the miracle of this cellular event. In the activation of aerobic respiration, positively charged protons accumulate within the mitochondrial intermembrane; this creates a dam of energy potential with a value equivalent to an electrical field strength of 30 million volts per metre or, to you and me, a lightning bolt. It's a wonder that with each breath, this delicate reaction doesn't end in a barbeque.

The Universe's magnificence is subjective; without another universe at our fingertips to benchmark, we're hard-pressed for a point of comparison. Of course, we're always welcome to measure nature's genius against the accomplishments of our species. No need to poke fun at science here; pitting Nobel contributions against creation is no fair match, but it underlines the point that our innovative exploits pale against nature's design and execution. Yet, we're still confident of the absence of a higher power. And, FYI, the intelligent design argument, or at least its most recent iteration, is virtually identical to the full-fat ontological position, the only material difference being the marketing department over at ID HQ has quietly redacted the mention of a 'Creator,' much more en vogue.

Not to seem ungrateful for the immense contributions by Lamarck, Malthus or Darwin to our understanding of natural evolution; however, much of what we've been offered approximates an inventory of events. From archaeology's deepest excavation point, scientists have theorised what may have happened, to whom and when (to the nearest 5 million years). With all that insight, pray-tell, which way leads me to the why and the how? Cells don't just become animated agents of life without the spark of ignition. The life sciences are a chronicle of flat theories that say nothing of that which incarnates this manuscript. No matter how comprehensive our knowledge of Earth's apparatus, we remain lightyears away from answering the most fundamental questions.

Humanity's relentless search for truth parallels nature's evolutionary drive for fitness. We could be rifling through a steaming landfill or seated comfortably pondering aesthetics; either way, nature hurtles towards us, dispatching her latest software update, life-changing surgery and not a whiff of anaesthetic. Her favourite instruments, inescapable suffering combined with a consciousness of time, in that order. Pain to spotlight our flaws and a finite lifespan with an unknown endpoint to ensure we pay attention. This game is not only designed; it is designed by an incomprehensible intelligence. The nexus of Man and nature's relationship is set on something far more profound than reproductive efficiency. This, ladies and gents, is a dance to enlightenment.

Design of Morality

The subject of morality demonstrates one of the closest convergences of atheism and spirituality. Admittedly, a flare of irritation stirs as I see modern philosophers reassign moral nuggets of ancient texts to prop up theories of ethics. And this is no isolated incident; they're all at it, from the cold-hearted physics of cause and effect to the daylight piracy of philosophers who find it acceptable to restitch Abrahamic teachings as their original revelations. The cheek of it. Of course, there's no IP on loving thy neighbour, but at least spare a mention of its etymology. Just basic respect, no? Though I get it; if it doesn't up the utility score, utilitarians have no use for respect or any other virtue. We'll specifically address those who float with 19th-century English philosopher Jeremy Bentham's utilitarian ethics. Broadly, utilitarianism measures the moral value of an action/inaction by the net happiness it produces for the greatest number of beneficiaries.

Here's the good news: Princeton bioethics Prof. Peter Singer is a prominent utilitarian philosopher who has occasionally garnered controversy for his views. In facilitating moral decision-making, those views have more than flirted with objectifying the value of sentient beings. Wince I may, but still, I understand that assessing the value of all players and outcomes is necessary and unavoidable in the scientific reduction of moral dilemmas. And before we get too sanctimonious, don't we all cast unconscious judgements upon every interpersonal encounter? At least this thought experiment is conscious. Singer's reasoning brings much-needed excitement to this debate, no matter how off-colour his take. I credit him and those in his academic lineage for demanding that we mortals engage thoughtfully with our conscience on what we believe and, more importantly, why.

Nevertheless, utilitarianism slips from the rational to the amoral without even noticing. This subject makes my skin crawl, so let's dive right in. Utilitarian morality fails because it commits a cardinal error by presupposing that everything is objectifiable in the name of ethical discourse. But not everything is. Harvesting the vital organs of one completely healthy individual in order to save five terminally ill individuals is the kind of morality that puts Satan on notice. Computational solutions do not dignify or apply to the unique human experience; this lack of ethical substance leaves the individual detached from conscience. Right here is the difference between a morality based upon love and truth versus a sterile decision-making process. How could consequentialists not foresee this flaw? Whilst fashioning their morals, they ignored the necessity of a centrifugal force, God. This kind of cringe is reminiscent of corporate middle management thinking they can fudge it without the vision of a CEO by endlessly tweaking the operating strategy. Utilitarians have reduced a spiritual endeavour into yet another economics drill.

But there is treasure here. Imagine a line-up of people from every walk of life on the spectrum of success (however you define it), see them and their faces, then place a plaque above each of their heads. Even when blank, the plaque makes us feel uncomfortable. Now ask yourself, is there anything that could be inscribed on that plaque that could remedy this discomfort? I doubt it. There is no price to quiet our soul because the intrinsic value of a life is infinite. Hell, we can't even tolerate the plaque when it's blank. It hurts because we are divine, yet the very existence of the plaque suggests otherwise; it implies that our value can be measured and exchanged and that humanity is wide open to this. Scenes of human trafficking have played out in all corners of history, and today, in some places, life is sold for less than nothing, but that's a question of currency and markets, not of intrinsic value. The fortune within is infinite, a concept too luminous for those who must account for everything.

We should thank the rational atheists who have gone to great lengths to argue that moral code is the only benefit of religious texts. However, the grave irony here is that in doing so, they prove the counterargument. When we are being crucified by tragedy, in those moments, we are not interested in pamphlets on mindfulness. At that point, we have descended into a world far beyond the reach of logic. The pain at those depths is unconscionable. Have you ever felt so desperately hurt that equalising the wrong just wouldn't cut it? This kind of hurt transforms lives and, many times, ends them.

In Khartoum, some years ago, my father's much younger cousin walked into the centre of her family's afternoon tea gathering. She stood directly in front of her mother's view, doused herself in gasoline and lit her body aflame. When I first heard this story, I was perplexed. Why would anyone choose such an agonising end over a swift, private exit? How naive. I had forgotten, or buried, the memory of not only wanting to die but to die several times over. At that point, it is no longer suicide. More accurately, it is a violent murder of the self, and that's what an anger of that magnitude will do. She must have been nineteen and dreamt of enrolling in an IT course at the local university. However, her mother intended to marry her off, so she put a stop to her procrastinating. And in return, the girl put an end to it all.

Here's to illustrate the total irrelevance of science and even religion in those climactic primal moments. There's a blockade on logic and even prayer; language cannot translate this darkness. At that moment, there is only the individual's insufferable pain and the Universe, God. Without God, there is no anchor to pull us through our metamorphosis. When bent double on the event horizon, our smarts are bloody redundant. By rejecting God, secular philosophers, therefore, expose the pitiful limits of moral reasoning. They have erased the inherent love and truth which underwrite moral codes. Love and truth are not some trite, *nice to have*; they root the principles, ensuring that when (not if) the philosopher's computations fail, we're not left barking at the moon. Tampering with ethics as though it's just another Game Theory proves that utilitarians cannot fathom the sacred ground they spoil.

As we'll demonstrate in the next section, while some things can be rigged, human experience is off the table. Atheist decision theories depend on probabilistic means to determine moral action; however, we cannot guarantee the roll of a die, let alone the correct move in a crisis. What is guaranteed is the nature of our intention; the focus on intent, for better or worse, keeps us authentic. And if nothing else, it ensures we respect virtues not as tools but intrinsically so. We believe in and are fortified by our morals; in other words, we stay good for our conscience and society because it matters whether an actor is deliberately ethical or if their good deed is just a quaint by-product of self-interest. A world governed by rationality absent of love is indifferent to which version of hell manifests, so long as it's fun for the majority. I aim for the good because no matter the outcome, it is the only way to love myself.

Design of Suffering

We needn't pore over Schopenhauer to agree that suffering is simply unavoidable; resignation to this reality is unanimous. However, the real question is how suffering and our expectance of suffering occur with striking certainty at the macro level of human experience, no less. How can this be viewed as anything less than impossible? Impossible because if existence is meaningless and our world is nothing more than the sum of arbitrary incidents occurring from the quantum to the cosmic, then given the odds, how is it that we all (civilisations across time, that is) suffer inescapably?

The inequalities we experience are vast and marked broadly by intellectual competence, genetics, character, culture, family, finances, social networks, nutrition, health, education, local geology, technology, the strength and stability of domestic/international politics, etc. This list shoots from the hip, and still, it's damn long. Of course, depending on one's perspective, there's much more or less which defines the quality of life. Indeed, there are more subjective markers, including purpose, freedom/s, love, and so much more. The point here is to illustrate the spectrum of ways in which 8 billion of us get indiscriminately served our starting net worth, and this is succeeded by ever-fluctuating circumstances and their corresponding effects, which add up to reality. Despite the countless opportunities to cultivate all versions of sustained happiness over a lifetime, somewhere in the wash, we became accustomed to the expectation that we will all suffer continuously - regardless of the circumstances we've been dealt or come to achieve. Indeed, if existence is meaningless and random, then at least some of us, maybe the best of us, or just one of us, could outsmart the pains of life. But that's not the case, is it? So how do we reconcile the fact that not one of us has ever managed to consistently predict or evade the surprising challenges of life or even achieve a modicum of sustained happiness? Life always has the last laugh. Isn't that curious?

Furthermore, how might we account for the uncanny correlation that binds our weaknesses to the custom-fit lessons we are subjected to? Science, poised to dispirit us at every corner, is ever thrilled to reduce the beauty of this synchronicity to yet another shade of dominos. It won't hold, but let's roll with it; science might argue that if you cannot learn a particular life lesson, it stands to reason that you'll suffer pains of a similar vein, as the chink in your character remains exposed and therefore susceptible to provocation. However, whilst this might predict the causal sequence from the individual's perspective, it fails to explain and, in fact, offers no explanation whatsoever regarding the other half of this equation. When the world meets us, wherever we happen to be, with events that instigate our individual growth, it does so with a precision of timing far beyond the science of frivolous chance. Furthermore, the uniqueness of the lesson's content, structure, and pivotal impact is curated exquisitely.

Cynically, we're so amused by our resistance to learn, wrapped up in the nostalgia of our flawed selves, that we altogether miss the true wonder of the upcoming retrial. Life delivers the same lesson with a brand-new cast and context. Still, the wisdom of the final act impales with a déjà vu so humbling that, at this moment, there's no space to contemplate the perfection of this phenomenon. How often can we cite statistical chance, a punt so budget, to settle the enigma of moral ontogenesis? We have an abundance of anthropologic literature detailing the environmental conditions for socialisation. However, when pinned on a far more pressing question, the exacting design of the individuation process, science takes the bench. Never gets old. If we keep shirking the questions that matter, we'll sound as ridiculous as the religious lot.

Transcendental Goals

Atheism is uncomfortably silent when the moment arises to present a profound and enduring vision for the individual or the collective. And, no, the biological survival of the species will not come close to cutting it; this is an evolutionary process, not a compelling vision. Beyond the grind of this hapless experience on our dear planet, we need something to aspire to, to dream of, an elevator pitch of sorts, to sustain our resolve.

It's rather embarrassing we're still at this point, given that scientists have philosophers and psychologists in their backyard, from Socrates to Peterson, asserting that the individual needs an inspirational vision or purpose whereby he may dock his self-actualisation. Scientists confined by analytical thinking might profit considerably by paying closer attention to the observations rendered by their less inhibited peers. It is, after all, the philosophers and psychologists who can peer through the conceptual limits of physical laws and social structures. For their mission, they are owed our respect and engagement.

Cynicism flourishes in the absence of a higher vision or a benevolent God-keeping score at our side through life's monotony, tragedy, and exhaustion. Should I strap up and make it my mission to settle every infraction since divine retribution is only a fairy tale? Should I indulge every urge to cross every moral and legal line I can get away with? Should I, when suffering exceeds the bounds of my tolerance, jump off the nearest multi-story? Should I tell my children there is no God? Don't hope for anything beyond the material; you're alone forever. All you have is your imagination; just don't imagine God.

God is Irreplaceable

Atheists hastily dispensed with the concept of God and soon found themselves all lost at sea. God occupies an unquantifiable space within the soul of humanity. In the run-up to the Enlightenment era, God as a concept was already being phased out of political discourse. However, removing God presented a new problem: designating a sovereign. Until today, political manifestos come up empty at the apex of their hierarchical models, and their recourse? To nominate a sorry stand-in for God: a king or a cabinet. Of course, they dare not openly admit that they're backfilling a space recently vacated by an irreplaceable force. Recognising the significance of this void would falter upon acknowledging the importance of that which filled it.

This quandary appears throughout the 16th and 17th centuries. British philosopher Thomas Hobbes explored the idea of a state without central governance; he set a rather bleak scene, which is unsurprising given his grim judgement of human nature. To ensure a functional society, Hobbes' development of Social Contract Theory asserts that the sovereignty of the citizens must be transferred and entrusted to a centralised governing entity that would rule the nation in absolute terms. However, this is where his projection comes undone; the sovereign, the king, is also a corruptible human. Therefore, how will the sovereign balance the order of rule whilst contending with his fluctuating moral temperament? How will the citizens endorse the legitimacy of a leader who cannot represent their interests and values faultlessly? As Hobbes uncovered, structural reform is far simpler than casting a sovereign.

Hobbes' miscalculation is in his personification of sovereignty. Sovereignty only gains legitimacy when ascribed to God. No human truly believes that any other human holds power over them; the individual's sovereignty is second to none. We may hum to the national anthem or oblige the tax man, but neither atheist nor believer buys the legitimacy of invented hierarchies. God is the one that credibly and consistently meets the moral ideal of the sovereign. Sporting the crown of absolute power is no picnic without omniscience, omnipresence, and omnipotence. Of course, the king could rule with his version of absolute power; however, in the interest of longevity, he must represent the citizens' ideal of the moral good. The stability of the monarchy is anchored to the reputation of the incumbent monarch. It's quite a pity that anxiety consumed Hobbes; if it weren't for his observable neurosis, we could have credited him for stealthily reorienting the reader to the divine. *Leviathan* would have been scored a satirical masterpiece which skilfully defined impossible criteria for a sovereign entity to which no human being could ever qualify.

Today, that vacancy is occupied by all shades of bad actors, a spiritual landfill for social media, tribal warfare, and fill-in-the-mindless blanks... In the West, when religion was still in fashion, the restrictions on society and science may have been excessive. But freedom in excess has brought us no closer to home. Despite the rigidity of former times, at least there was a sense of substance grounding us. Now, minorities have become caricatures, and news of climate change headlines daily. We would literally rather chase the wind than deal with child trafficking, global poverty, or anything that hurts to confront. Of course, Gen Y tailed the one cause that demands the least amount of work - *sorry, had to.* Make no mistake: this generation is seeking God. They could have chosen any moral cause; the United Nations offers 17 distinct Sustainable Development Goals, but Gen Y chose the environment, as they seek to believe in and defend a virtuous, omnipotent, ever-present and immortal power.

Unconvincing Agents of Atheism & Religion

The extremes of both camps are ridden with pride and absurdity. Religious wars rage on unaffected by space, time, or reason, as do the exploits of clergymen who abuse with impunity. Meanwhile, science's abject rejection of anything beyond empirical evidence is hella lazy. Dumping civilisations' worth of suffering at the door of religion is an unbelievable lack of self-awareness. Might we pull up the clippings on secular tyrants such as Stalin, Hitler, Mao or even future AI? Frankly, the body count shames us all, no matter the cause, so let's end the antagonism.

If we're not ready for reconciliation, at least we can reconcile with the truth. The evil we suffer is manmade. Moral philosophers include natural catastrophes and disease in their definition of evil; however, this is a misappropriation of the term. Such unfortunate occurrences are devastating, but they carry an essence of neutrality. Of course, there could be a spiritual connection to disease, such as a stress-induced cardiac event; however, there's still a level of moral detachment between the event and its victim. The nature of the evil perpetrated by humans, however, is far from impersonal. Shakespeare captured the pains of love, betrayal, and power, to name a few. I doubt our appreciation of his works could have been equalled with literature that romanticised earthly disasters. We are the source of our own suffering. Not communism, not the devil, nor the jihadi; these are agents of evil, monikers if you will, but their relevance pales against the evil within. Evil is mostly invited through avoiding the unresolved and, therefore, self-inflicted. We humans perpetrated every malevolent act recorded in history; we are the common denominator. Whether it's too much or too little of God, it doesn't seem to affect the bonfire, does it?

Questions of creation or the afterlife? Convincing conclusions, I see none, but worse, both sides lack the humility to acknowledge where their positions promptly run out of rope. Judging by their confidence, you'd be forgiven for assuming they've lived this life a thousand times. Moreover, neither camp explains the point of this existence. Dear atheists, 'nothing' is not an answer. And believers, why did God create all this instead of, say, doing nothing - as atheists suggest, only to still end up with a universe? Right. I'm more critical of atheism because empiricism doesn't tolerate grey areas. Nonetheless, this question plays on my mind; however, I do not expect to be spoon-fed all the answers. And, *no*, that's not a cop-out; my children feel knowledgeable and powerful, yet they haven't the faintest notion of their ignorance. The world will update their understanding as and when they are ready.

History is rife with examples of so-called spiritual leaders who fail to represent their beliefs fairly, from the intimidating sheikh who insists you swallow each verse of the Quran without a word since meaningful debate is tantamount to blasphemy. Or to the ridiculous Jehovah's Witness whose whole get-up is as pitiful as the travelling salesman. Men of Abrahamic cloth commit to publicised debates without any intention of engaging. No integrity, no skin in the game. Too arrogant or ignorant to trust in the possibility that the exchange could light a new direction. If they would just trust the process, we needn't witness another overblown priest get served his Holy Communion on primetime. The debate is treated as something of a charade, and so it is.

Atheists, with their bag of tricks, ready to disorient the best of us, explaining procedural biological death in murderous detail because, of course, they've experienced it. This, whilst mind-numbing, at least one can postulate a defence without fear of igniting Armageddon, as with the inexorable believer. Mind you, there will always be a solid tranche of inexorable atheists who simply object to any form of authority at home or the office, and God is no exception. Given the value and necessity of such discourse, a stalemate is a hard loss for us all.

Miracles & Awe

Research by American professor of psychology Dr Dacher Keltner extensively demonstrates the scientific effect of awe upon the human condition. I find it hard to separate the spiritual from miracles and awe, but I accept that for some, such experiences start and finish in the body. Christ, we do know how to spoil the few moments worth living for.

Now, I promised to keep it street, so let's dig in on the more common type of awe experienced through learning. When describing awe, many attest to sensing tranquillity, silence, unity, the immateriality of time, and more. A compelling exchange between consciousness, genetics, and circuitry is revealed when we achieve a milestone understanding.

Relive the sensation experienced from a past moment when you identified the solution to a novel problem. Laser in on the moment the problem is about to be solved, the moment you silence everything, including your breath, when crossing the boundary from ignorance to knowledge, that download is served with a physiological rush that is transcendent, but why? Indeed, if this is the first time we've encountered this challenge, how do we know with unquestionable certainty that we're right? Shouldn't we confer with a paper, peer or teacher before activating reward systems? Of course, that's not necessary. We know we're right. We always knew. Rechavi et al. didn't need to bury generations of roundworms only to prove that ancestral data is in fact, heritable. It's clear our journey is not just one of discovery but of rediscovery. So, what is it that operates at quantum speeds, with bullet-proof confidence, painting the town red whilst our rational mind tries to catch up? Combining consciousness with the genetic archive is no match for pure logic. If that is not a spiritual experience, then I rest my case.

Fear of Death

OK, so this is a question to atheists. If we consider the fear of death, it's broad and subjective, so we will narrow the focus down to the simple fact that life is ending, excluding adjacent issues such as the time of death or how we die. The fear of death in an atheist frame of reference just doesn't add up. Where's the rationality in fearing death without God or an afterlife? Moreover, how is the idea of the before life any more frightening than the end of life? And given that we have already been through our uneventful pre-life condition, it stands to reason our post-life state should be just as flat. This fear of death is quite telling; it implies a doubt that the pre-life condition was far from uneventful, only forgotten.

My father was born a Muslim and then lived a life in service to science, adamant nothing awaited on the other side. On his final day, he died believing in God. Please understand this was not a choice; asking him if he believed in God would have been absurd. In those few days, he was having a spiritual encounter. It was not a hallucination, hard to describe; he was not an observer; he was already part of something transcendent. Asking him if he believed in God would have rung like asking if he was human. We watched this great man who had lived for empirical discipline go home to his maker with such certainty in the next chapter and the regret of a life half-lived. The life and soul of every party, he would spontaneously recite Oscar Wilde, then laugh uncontrollably at a joke from a Christmas cracker. I imagine him now chiming in as I embark on my first book, "Dear girl, won't you think of the trees?" He could cut and charm in one stroke. This man was pure magic, with a Ph.D. in statistics, a senior position in the UN, a political revolutionary, and his first love, Chivas Regal, in his briefcase on his last ambulance trip. I could see he wished he'd let the light in sooner than palliative care, not for any religion, just to have lived open to a universe of knowledge and not in a constant state of defence of science. At his end, there was no believing or not believing; only the final acceptance that 'nothing' could never have been the answer.

Proof

Isn't it curious that we roast believers for retreating when pressed on the provability of their beliefs, yet there's no such symmetry for atheists? An even critique is essential, but this is more serious. The stakes are high because our understanding of physical reality is entrusted to science; still, it receives a fraction of said criticism for the divergence of classical and quantum physics. And if not that, then this: cosmologists have been in a back-and-forth on the nature of the Universe. We hear that its charge, spin (of its objects) and mass come to a net total of zero; it appears flat, without a centre or an edge; the jury's out on its beginning, and it has no definitive end or at least none our instruments can reach. Combine this with the fact that we're made up of immortal atoms mainly constituted of space, and if it wasn't for the constant movement of subatomic particles, who knows where or what we'd be? So then, would it be too much to ask that we prove the reality we're all debating even exists before we set sail on the God question? The burden of proof is placed inordinately high only where it suits us; nevertheless, this is my favourite argument for the existence of God, and it's real simple.

The following must be some of the most common unanswered challenges from your average Joe Blow: *If God is real, where is he when we need him? How could the Almighty while away eternity binge-watching this melodrama, and is it much of a page-turner when he knows the plot? If God exists, why doesn't he settle this maddening debate and present himself once and for all?* Easy. If God is God, perhaps the teacher, and I am the student here to be enlightened or, at the very least, a little less of the me that seems routinely compelled to piss in my own soup, and this universe is the school, then what is the course?

Faith. Faith in ourselves and the promise of a better existence is not cultivated through empirical proof of the divine but through sinking into those gracious moments that lift us out of our despair strengthened. Or when we achieve something so extraordinary and that same energy, unequivocally the signature of God, feels so palpably close that our whole being is levitating with happiness, or - is it gratitude? In those overwhelming moments of deep gratitude, it's hard for atheists to explain the nature and source of this humbling feeling we are all subjected to. The moment joy turns to gratitude, who are you thanking? Are we thanking the Universe, our higher selves, or is it God? Not only for coming through and delivering our shabby dreams. No, deeper. In that moment, I thank God for proving his very existence and even my own. We feel seen, counted, here and loved. Evidence appears after faith, not before; equations resolve after faith, not before. Without suffering and faith, there would be no story to tell; this world would be a museum. Faith is a powerful force more convincing than any data a sceptic could pray for.

For the Sport

I cannot help but notice the uncanny correlation between the Abrahamic and the scientific creation accounts; roll with me. God and science agree that in the beginning, before any bang, the Universe was empty space or "...void and formless...." Then the protons met the electrons to form hydrogen, and we heard the words, "Let there be light," and then "There was light." Astronomers insist the sun came before the Earth;

however, given we're talking of a 57m-year difference between the age of our Solar System and the Earth, both of which are measured on a scale of multiple billions, this might not be the hill to die on. Next, the "Sky," or the beginnings of Earth's atmosphere, developed during the Hadean to Archean aeons. This was followed by the Proterozoic aeon, God's land, seas and vegetation, and we're still in step. Then boom, enter the Cambrian Explosion, 538m years ago; fossil records show a sudden appearance of complex life. Crucially, we are still missing evidence of the precursors to this fauna, i.e., fossils on the same gradient. The Cambrian records agree with God that complex life came about vastly and swiftly. However, this historical punctuation doesn't sit well with evolutionary biologists; they would prefer that fossils evidence evolution, not a standing start. God created the "... creatures of the seas ... and winged birds ..." followed by animals and Man. Palaeontologists almost agree; however, they'd prefer birds to evolve from dinosaurs, so they stick to their original story despite evidence of bird fossils and footprints from the Triassic era.

The Universe's inflation started around Earth's beginning, 4.543 billion years ago, round about the same time God had his falling out with Lucifer. He was cast down to Earth, and the battle for human consciousness was on. At that point, dark energy started to overpower gravity, pulling matter or us apart. Lucifer warned God that he would convince Man there was no God, at which point it was open season. And here we are, Netflixing in our atheist jammies, pondering the wonder of AI, which we created in our own image; naturally, we wouldn't want to veer off-script, would we? Atheists might consider distancing themselves from the predictions of religious texts that, in this world, play out like clockwork.

Consciousness: Motherboard or the Portal?

At the outer limits of the brain's processing capacities rests our final defence, consciousness. And in the toss-up between rationality and morality (no, dear utilitarians, they are not the same), consciousness is society's last defence. We each and all reap the spoils of consciousness, a self-governance beyond intellect that rescues us from the excesses of intellect, a consciousness of truth, love and freedom.

Modern neuroscience has been engaged in a taxing cat and mouse with consciousness through the exploration of the brain and spine. Physicists confront the *Hard Problem of Consciousness* when asked to explain its emergence: how do unconscious fundamental particles combine to form conscious human beings or unconscious rocks? Not knowing the what, where, when, how and never mind the why prompts us to consider how we have accepted any scientific assumptions about consciousness at all. Attempting to locate consciousness in a physical structure is as tragic as looking for love inside a Valentine's card. The card may be made with love, signed in love, and sent with love, but it can never be love.

Consciousness is so much more than being awake, feeling or comprehending. It is my highest expression of conscience, my avenue to God. Consciousness remains pristine. However, its freedom of expression depends upon our physical and emotional health. Consciousness navigates the perils of a fluctuating cerebral state; when this is disturbed or scarred by emotional trauma, drugs, injury and more, consciousness facilitates the restoration of balance. Memory can ease or obstruct consciousness, particularly the amygdala, which hosts emotionally intense content of the individual's life story and beliefs. This powerful narrative influences the selection of incoming data. The constant negotiation between these forces thoroughly amuses me, how a skinhead turns and almost smiles at me before his narrative reminds him he's a Klansman. Love those; they're the best! His consciousness spends the rest of the night refereeing his memory and conscience before he defaults into misalignment.

Cognitive psychologist Donald Hoffman and his team at the University of California are challenging our understanding of our perception of reality, particularly spacetime. Their findings illustrate that we interpret a fraction of the available stimuli, and that fraction is invited on the condition that it synergises with our evolutionary goals. Consciousness must contend with a brain whose cognitive processes may or may not be operating in the spiritual interests of the individual and perhaps even divergent from objective reality itself.

Despite its necessity, change is challenging and significant change harder still; a shift of perspective is not merely a labour of filing. A new opinion in one branch of thought arrives decked with renovation implications for a spectrum of others. Furthermore, the impact of these changes may begin with neural chemistry; however, they potentially end in a transformation of the individual's material or relational circumstances; consciousness must steer this resistance. Consciousness must counsel, heal, and on the rare occasion it is invited, light the way.

As a child, I always wondered why it was acceptable to God that some societies would be informed of his message by virtue of a postcode lottery, but others, not so much. I've come to understand that on some level, no matter how slowly or painfully, consciousness intimately teaches us all. To this end, it is God, not religion that is always with us, just at the other end of a thought.

Conclusion

You'll notice that we haven't seriously discussed the Universe's origins; this omission was deliberate. Forgive my scepticism, but projections 13.8 billion years out? The accruing margin of error blows straight through any tokens of plausibility. And to the other camp, religious stories on this one come off whimsical at best, sorry. Frankly, what difference does it make at the individual level? Establishing the validity of the Big Bang may shed light on long-standing assumptions, ultimately flipping the script or granting greater coherence to present-day science. There's no overstating the value of proof in that context. However, when the creation story is weighed by its moral relevance to you and me in the here and now, we might agree that research dollars could be better spent.

We're partly to blame for the pressure scientists find themselves subjected to. The world expects a continuum of impeccable data and iron-cast solutions to life's challenges, no excuses. In 2021, at 38, I underwent spinal surgery to alleviate a herniated calcified disc; yes, that hurt. My surgeon was not your run-of-the-mill physician full of doubt and forgettable tips. Oh no, Harty communicated in cold, hard bullet points without a spoonful of anything. A heavy-metal biker in his free time, not that it mattered, but I just enjoyed meeting a white coat brave enough to let their personality breathe and one that was direct, even at the expense of customer service.

He consistently projected confidence and certainty until a few days before my operation. I could see he was putting off a conversation; I just hadn't realised it was ours until the next appointment. He looked hot, but it was November. I watched a visibly distressed Harty with curiosity. Given his usual whatevs, don't own a clipboard swag, I wondered what it could be. As he fevered up and stammered through, I heard something resembling "...the standard risks..." What a relief; he was only rehashing the disclaimer. Assured that this was a spell of the night-before jitters, I looked him straight in the eye, and he knew it was time to cut the crap.

Finally, he drew a breath, and as he exhaled, I reminded him, "You are not God. You're a doctor." Harty looked at me, so relieved like he'd just been granted an extra week to complete his school homework. It didn't interest me that he most certainly did not believe in God. That was irrelevant because his entire demeanour confirmed that neither surgical tenure, license, peer esteem, nor any other accolade could ever close the final gap between that which he is and that which he could never be. Of course, soulless surgeons exist and do a better job of concealing their anxiety, but their arrogance doesn't put a dent in that gap. At the best of times, our competence is uncertain, and our certainty is mostly absent.

The limits of science are most evident to those on the outside looking in. Science sold us on abandoning God, citing faith as untestable and too subjective to accommodate, no room in this *inn*. They sold it, we bought it. The responsibility is mutual. Nevertheless, given the continued knowledge gaps, it blows my mind that science gained so much credibility in the last few decades. Astoundingly, we can barely chime in on 5% of the observable Universe or the 80% yet to be explored of our oceans, never mind the poles, forests, deserts, bacteria, the internet or even the origin of our next damn thought! With all that's missing, how do we warrant the brazen arrogance in academia? James Webb could probe every parsec of our cosmos, and we'd still be flustered by data that has zero interest in humouring our instruments or theories. Perhaps God deliberately keeps us suspended in the dark? Our round-the-clock ignorance may eventually humble the bots amongst us; this could be just the buttering up we've always needed in readiness for God's immense and invisible love. Here's hoping.

Of course, I'm being too judgy. Science is a marvel, but arrogance invites judgment. In any case, science and atheism should expect to take some heat for the wreckage levelled by their assault on faith. Look where we are. Responsibility was once honoured; now, our feelings rule the roost, measured in real-time, of course! Legal reforms trace our fleeting whims, corporations seek to cultivate a 'sense of belonging' (wonder who they're missing?), and social media swallows our young whole. Technology, convenience, vaccines, free sex, change sex; none of it can lower the pitch of our grief. Where's the spirituality that anchored individuals to truth, discipline, purpose, and family? Atheism is the religion of the free. Free of conscience, free of God, free of the shame that none of this worked. Yet still, we should kneel to prescription drugs and play another episode. Is this the promised land? How could we betray ourselves so profoundly? Consumption and the pursuit of fuck all.

Who knows precisely when the tables turned, but here we are, watching these so-called debates as science gives religion the dressing down of the century. Whether this reversal stings or soothes, religion must take responsibility for science's snotty hubris. Faith in science galvanised in the centuries that bookended the Age of Reason despite delivering no further evidence against the existence of God. Nevertheless, the liability for this one is duly set. The rational ego was borne of the Church's grandiosity. This new world order answered religion's unchecked intimidation, judgement, corruption and, above all, its refusal to share the stage. With confidence renewed, the Enlightenment endowed the emergent generations with the spoils of industrial and human rights development. However, these perks couldn't cover the untold cost of pulling the plug on religion.

With greater precision, society might have added spiritual enlightenment to its credentials by only reserving impeachment for the bad actors of the cloth. Instead, we wrote a blank check on the write-down of the metaphysical. Mikhail Bulgakov's *Master & Margarita* is a modern prophecy on an atheist's paradise; believing in nothing only means we fail to recognise the darkness when it seizes humanity. Today we believe in the greatest evils but refuse to believe in the greatest good. The centuries that followed the Enlightenment would see us gorge on freedom and divorce our soul, only to search for it in all corners and almost find it in something called consciousness.

Did you ask yourself where God is? Regardless of one's beliefs, it's not a simple exercise. Reflecting on this, I sense that God is most evident within my conscience. That flash of sympathy my husband tries to repress on a Friday night. Dinner arrives, and he's faced with deciding the tip. Reaching for less than he should, he's met at the door by a delivery driver 15 years his senior and the weight of regret. Classic. If it weren't for God in these moments, there would be no moment; we'd flatline in apathy or, worse, ration kindness with an eye on its rate of return. Without God, we are AI.

God is our sacred confidant, if only we'd extend our trust. Generous with love and unsparing with the truth, this may not cushion all blows, but it will relieve us of the emptiness. However, growth is necessary; one of God's artful designs is in the setup that pits homeostasis against our insatiable drives. We pursue, and we suffer. God allowing us to suffer is a beautiful gift. We live free. Free to pursue a life of love and truth, or we can grind on blaming a God we don't believe in for all the suffering we have inflicted upon one another. Come on now.

Pooling our Resources

In terms of historical subscription, God outsells everything. That fact in and of itself cannot be pinned on the ignorance of human civilisation. There is zero empirical proof that concludes the existence or non-existence of the metaphysical. Regardless, God wins the soul of humanity. Some believe, some don't, but we all seek a truth to return to. Perhaps we could work with this energy.

Imagine a future for this civilisation whereby we advance less burdened by our philosophical commitments. Scholars of the sciences and humanities would vacate previously held notions of one another, perhaps even respect one another, if not for their present knowledge, then by the glaring mutual limits of their intelligence. If medical boards would ally with or extend an invitation to spiritual insights, who knows where that could lead? As it applies to health, stress is the intersection of the material and the spiritual. Emotions impact biology: on that, we can all agree. This is the fundamental point, perhaps the only point at which these two worlds meet. Whether its adrenals revving up for some high-stakes event, a silent heart attack at the loss of love, or chronic inflammation, the insidious cost of drifting from who you know you could be. If the effects of stress are analogous to sugar and smoking, there must be another route to prevention and cure that does not include a prescription. A collab between these rivals might sound like a reach, but it's already begun. The secular practice of meditation, speaking affirmations, and preserving a state of gratitude are all forms of prayer.

There's no chalking all the strife of the last two decades to the erosion of faith. However, fractures within us and across Western democracies have recently magnified, but not beyond recourse. As a Millennial (just), I still remember when journalism was a respectable occupation, with correspondents selected for the strength of their intellect and impartiality. In those times, we debated politics unreservedly at the dinner table, religion, sadly not enough. Reproductive education was not an opportunity to sexualise school children; no, that would have been grooming. And the presence of masculine energy was truly valued. Perhaps an open dialogue between politics and spirituality could reorient this cultural drift. Several world affairs raised here are stranded in a political dead heat; there's a distinct inertia and lack of courage to resolve sensitive disputes.

Science and spirituality depend on truth; and since Woke culture undermines truth, science and spirituality may reunite in its defence. A return to a belief in something greater would restore a good part of that impetus to improve our world by accepting uncomfortable truths. In the final analysis, we have one problem and one problem alone: the abandonment of the soul, of God. The rest are symptoms.

When physics and metaphysics blend their insight to address the existential mysteries, global suffering and the direction of civilisation, that'll be a future worth contemplating.

CHAPTER II

ABORTION

ABUSE | HOMELESSNESS | TRAFFICKING | SUICIDE

*Find me the one who dies of **natural** causes....*

The two-year-old Asian boy, my sweet friend, didn't know a word of Chinese, let alone English. He was overwhelmed with dread just by seeing the fear in my eyes and the tears streaming from my seven-year-old face. In less than a heartbeat, he understood from my state that I had been somewhere he shouldn't even try to imagine. Behind this cry were no survivors.

The boy lived on the ground floor of a low-rise block of flats in Cardiff, Wales; on the level above lived my abuser and his wife. It was a blistering day in the late 80s, and my single mother had handed me to my father for a short break during the summer holidays. As soon as he received me, he dropped me off to Osman, the devil himself.

I don't believe all paedophiles are pure evil and beyond redemption. However, Osman was just that. Until now, as I write, a grown woman in my early 40s; beyond the abuse, I have never understood why he went the extra mile to crush my spirit. I stayed with him and his clueless wife for over a week. Now and again, he would allow me to play with the kid downstairs; this allowed Osman to rewrite his Ph.D. so that it wouldn't resemble all the economic papers written and sold by my father to lazy African students. Plagiarism was no picnic in the 90s.

You're wondering how he crushed my spirit. That day, the sun roasted us all. Osman allowed me to play with the Chinese boy. We played toddler games, and for a time, I was content just to be safe, but then his sweet mother, hoping to invite a cool draft, opened both the flat door and the main building door. Once the boy saw his mother, I realised we would be taking a break from playing; he stood with both feet planted solidly on the ground and tapped his mother's chest bone as she knelt towards him. Starting to feed, he watched me from the side of his eye, never breaking his gaze. I wondered if maybe his mother could help me escape; she seemed so kind, and her eyes still had an innocence I had long lost. Stupid idea. She couldn't comprehend my English, and her naive efforts would push me deeper into hell. The mother leaves us to play, but this time, I'm not at all content; those thoughts of escape and idle strategising had left me ready to implode.

My last hope would be to get the boy to understand me. Perhaps he could translate for his mother? Perhaps all this time, he was pretending to be younger than he really was, with all that breastfeeding whilst standing. Even my young mind understood the potential upside of asking for help far outweighed the fear of failure. I held his sticky little hands before me, pierced his stupor with my stare, and begged him to understand. As he looked back at me, he suddenly looked much older, but like a dream, his conscience bailed. He knew he couldn't hear my story as that would involve walking voluntarily into hell. He retreated, a toddler again, and I alone again. No matter how I explained, he giggled continuously. Then I began to cry. There was no one to turn to, I didn't know the neighbours or the way home, I could not call home. I was trapped. It was the first time in my life that I distinctly remember crying like an adult; Christ, I cried so intensely. My whole being was a closed circuit; pain poured from me but would not leave me.

The sun beamed in through the window onto my round, teary face. It was the closest feeling to love I had experienced in a long time. I closed my eyes, my breathing slowed, and then I decided that if I wanted to be free, I would have to run. The building was positioned in the centre of a cul-de-sac, not that I had a plan; after all, I was dropped off by car, and this was the first time I'd been to his home. All the other times he'd stalked me, he visited my home, sometimes my mother would be napping in her room, and I'd be in the living room watching cartoons. She sometimes had to work or run errands, and he would be outside waiting for her to leave. Then, despite the double bolt on the 2-inch-thick door of our top-floor flat, he would kick and kick the door repeatedly, terrorising me. It was so excruciatingly loud that I would hide on the floor at the foot of my mother's bed, knees clenched, face down, tears seeping onto the tops of my long white socks and praying for the lock to hold, praying with everything I had, or everything that was still mine. The neighbour chastises him, and then he'd disappear. Just to be sure, I'd lay perfectly still on the ground and fall asleep until Mum was home.

Running was the only option, I reassured myself, looking out from the main entrance of his building. I jumped straight onto the front path and ran as fast as I could, hoping to see someone on their front lawn, washing their car or anything at all. On this beautiful blue-sky day, there was not a single soul who heard my scream. Now what? Should I knock on doors? But as I slowed to think, I heard his laugh. He was leaning on the entryway, clapping slowly, crisply, laughing loudly, celebrating my foolishness. I knew it was time to surrender. Maybe if I give in whilst he's still amused, I can join him laughing, split myself off, letting the Hurt laugh at the Hope. The Hurt was both his accomplice and mine; she would appear at times like this to give me a sense of control and him a sense of my resilience. Being all victim was too much to bear. She may have lightened the load, but this little charade was the ultimate betrayal.

As I reached the main door, he knelt to meet my gaze, stroked my hair, wiped my tears and asked me where I was running to. He was a visionary at finding new angles, and this one still burns today, "Don't you know, it was your parents who brought you to me?" his eyes lit up searchingly. The climax for this broken soul was when he could watch Hope break in real-time. You see, it was all for this moment, the abuse was mere paperwork. Then his words sunk in, and I assure you, I did everything possible not to give him another tear. But this was a whole new game that had to be lost several times before it was learnt. When I finally looked up, he saw my eyes. And he was born again. Osman thought those words would end my faith in the world, giving him full run on these bones. How naive. He had no idea of the love that pours from me but never leaves me.

Of course, this could happen to anyone, but often, the worst of it happens to the children of those who are not ready to be parents.

Meine Lieben,

Speaking as the un-aborted subject, I believe in the right to and necessity of legalised abortion.

Debate

Brass Tacks

The arguments for and against legalised abortion in the West have been beached without progress since I was a politics undergrad. Decades. Let's park the fringe aspects of this debate, which we could most likely reach a consensus upon with concerted effort. By 'fringe,' I refer to exceptional circumstances, for instance, cases whereby a pregnancy places the mother's health in serious jeopardy, impregnation due to sexual assault, or a non-existent social care system.

We will cut right to the ground that no one will surrender. Distilling this complex subject is essential to understanding why this topic is ricocheting back into political discourse. Fringe issues are loaded subjects that, when aimed correctly, have muzzled the opposition, allowing the Left to gain a substantial advantage in the abortion debate. But whilst downing their beet juice, we all missed the true victory of reconciling the core ideological conflict.

Agency

The pro-choicers have been spinning their wheels on the bodily integrity and autonomy position. The notion is the female is not defined or limited by her procreative value to society, moreover, her rights and interests are not secondary to her unborn child. She holds ultimate agency over her body; therefore, no being could develop within her without her continued consent. The cold reality is that no being can grow in their mother's womb without consent. There are innumerable ways in which she can damage or end that life intentionally or otherwise, and this applies long after birth, let alone during pregnancy. This isn't to state the obvious but to suggest a new starting point of physical reality, not of abstraction.

When considering the interests of other parties, this point is brought into sharp focus. What of the rights of those who must administer abortions against their instincts? City hospitals couldn't stay afloat without the support of temporary staff, so drafting in a nurse from another ward might make operational sense until she's frozen between God and her pay check. That sucks, but administrators are so far down the Christmas list they barely get a mention - and for good reason. Like it or not, there is a pecking order and ignoring it infuriates her at the top. Therefore, acknowledging the truth of this power imbalance between the mother and pro-life advocates might revitalise this debate. After all, negotiation is an art, and frankly, when was the last time we profited by vilifying the one holding all the power?

Timing

The critical moment an embryo becomes an ethical subject and, therefore, entitled to human rights is a deal-breaking point of contention. Both sides of the fence concede that the pre-birth child gains legal legitimacy at a certain point during the pregnancy. But on what premise and at which point exactly? Is it the moment, 'he came too soon'? And if so, does this wide net catch in vitro fertilisation (IVF) or stem cell research?

In the interest of saving lives, diseases and their respective treatments are modelled by stem cell researchers, and these experiments destroy embryos. Most are surplus IVF embryos that weren't up to par. Both industries are no strangers to waste; the UK's *Human Fertilisation & Embryology Authority's* 1991-2019 datasets recorded 3,106,319 embryos intended for IVF were in fact, destroyed. Most stem cell labs observe the 14-day embryo age guidelines, but there are a minority of countries that don't, continuing their research into the first heartbeats. Curiously, this receives much less attention than abortion. Furthermore, both sides unduly preference rights over outcomes, driving full speed past the pivotal argument that settles this debate, which I'll get to.

Sanctity

The defence of recognising the sanctity of life is a pro-life position that resonates profoundly with all of us. This principle comes close to perfection, and at the very least, it is the purest thread to the story rendered by the religious or right-wing vote.

In a universe where much of all experience is virtual, and we are indexed individually and collectively by our productive and, or consumer value, it is deeply heartening to be reminded that we, once upon a time, held intrinsic value. Whether or not we accept religious principles, this evokes an undeniable warmth, and we are humbled as we watch pro-lifers on the political battlefield benevolently defend our divine worth. They fight for our dignity, expecting nothing in return, which they'll get with sprinkles when we grow up and choose atheism.

Dead Pixels

Before addressing the root of this debate, two glaring misassumptions are latent in political and social discourse which simply need to be retired. Pro-lifers underpin their arguments with the premise that pregnant women seeking abortions diminish or wholly disregard the value of their unborn child. This dark assumption fuels the equally flawed fixture on the Left, which asserts that pro-lifers bear no interest towards the hapless foetus but seek to subjugate women using pro-life legislation. If both assumptions are true, then tragically, neither party cares for the child, and this is nothing more than a war of the sexes. Since the truth here is nebulous, allow me to rule this a breakdown in communication. Not only are both assumptions way off-target, but they also provide a toxic stage for the debate. Therefore, in the interest of good faith, a clean slate, and real progress, shall we at least try to assume that the opposing political camp is well-intentioned?

The Bill

To advance this discussion, let's reframe. I propose the critical determinant is not centred upon the pregnant woman's right to freedom of choice or the foetus' right to be incubated in whomever until birth. No. By concentrating on the consequences of prohibition and the potential outcomes for the unintended life, society might edge closer to what matters.

In a pro-life jurisdiction, the unborn child is by no means safe. Firstly, to live, the foetus must pray his mother resists the urge to visit an underground chop shop, of which there'll be many as this pop-up black market evolves. And that assumes she hasn't pulled her own 'home-ec' project to get the job done. Once the foetus survives those odds, he must develop within a highly stressed womb where he'll stew in cortisol for at least the first two trimesters. Touch down. A foster home welcomes the child; no skin-on-skin, no breastfeeding and no one to call Mum. Haunted for God knows how long by the cloud of rejection, mother couldn't cope, and father in the wind. I invite you to survey the mental health of those spun through the social care system, the ones who are still alive, that is. The stats on their prospects are eyewatering. And those could be the lucky ones who didn't come home with parents who had no business being parents. Though pro-choice, given my experience as an unwanted child who couldn't have been aborted within the Muslim community, but also as a mother who feels the foetus is an extension of her body, one entity, I still insist that pro-lifers shouldn't give up the ghost. This is a healthy and necessary debate, but to stay in the race, pro-lifers must radically strengthen their political approach.

Foetus rights? What about the child's rights? Disinterest in the child's well-being cuts the legs from the pro-life agenda and is precisely why the feminists believe this to be yet another slice of chauvinism. Radical reform of the institutions and the ecosystem that supports orphans is the only way to move this needle. Pro-lifers can start by evidencing their care through tangible improvements in foster care resources. Then they can pivot to the spiritual undercurrent which has contributed to the rise in abortions, a trend which has inverted much of the developed world's demographics. Why are we falling out of love with the prospect of having children?

Recognise the balance of power between mother and legislator, level up foster systems, and confront the culture which erodes the love of parenthood and the optimism in humanity. Starting there, we can work our way back to the debate table. Otherwise, we continue to bury the unborn, the orphaned, and history will bury the Right.

Conclusion

It was during my final year of university, shortly after my twenty-first birthday, that I was in the hospital. I remember the exact date because as I lay there trying to forget everything about the abortion pills I had just taken orally and the other end, my mother called, screaming to high heaven that I had forgotten her birthday. It was May seventh, two-thousand and four.

Six weeks earlier, days after taking the pregnancy test, I notified the doctor of my intent to abort. The NHS insisted I wait a few more weeks to ensure it *worked.* Counting the days was horrendous. The blame was all mine. Even so, marshalling the plumping up of the little guy ahead of his last day was something else. You can imagine the anxiety and depression that mounted up to the final appointment.

Predictably, the on-duty nurse disapproved of my choice to terminate. Although she could feel my despair and infer my circumstances, she still disapproved. I couldn't comprehend how, with the blessing of the Almighty, she stood in the way of the most loving act I could offer my unborn child. To that day, life had been a slow-motion gutting of everything worth living for. She stared at her screen, then her lap, and waited for me to read and sign the NHS contract. She didn't look at me for the entire day I was there.

Who started that ghastly rumour that abortions were just a pill as innocuous as the morning-after solution? Seriously. The nurse showed me to the ward of untouchables. I saw an Asian girl alone in the room next door; she cried all day. With me was my university boyfriend, Stuart, a kind pothead from a good family. He was the icing on the cake. If, even for a moment, I wavered over my decision (never happened, btw), I would just need to glance at Stuart's tragic existence and be right back on track. You see, I had lost hope but not faith. I was angry at God, even heartbroken, but still believed in him. Know why? Because none of it at any moment seemed random. All of it was personal. Only long after the trials, did I understand the lessons. But before that, I would throw my life away in protest. And given that trajectory, delivering my child would have been grossly negligent. As a child, I dreamed of celebrating my children, telling them we planned and prepared for their arrival and that they would be the centre of our world, not some by-product of religious or legal obligations.

My decision to terminate was an act of love and sacrifice. I forced myself that afternoon to see every piece of my 9-week foetus collected on the nurse's tray. This was so I would suffer the maximal trauma for my part in the devastation and, in exchange, receive the chance to grow up and become the decent and stable human being that a mother should be, and society desperately needs. The process, the scarring and the haunting; abortion is no drive-thru. The night I returned home, I dreamt of a crying baby; in the dream, I felt elated, as though I'd had the baby. Endorphins flushed through me as I ran to the perfectly made cot; it was empty and covered in blood. Every year or so, I get a visit in my dream from my boy; by now, he's almost 20. I talk, he listens, I ask for forgiveness and keep the promise I made that day in the hospital: to pursue a life of love and security, ensuring I need never contemplate abortion.

Trust in the mother's choice. She will suffer either way and forever, but the child need not.

CHAPTER III

DIVERSITY, THE ROAD TO JUSTICE

"If they are free, they are not equal. And if they are equal, they are not free."
- Aleksandr Solzhenitsyn

I was *born* a capitalist. Too much? Born a capitalist because we are compelled to one philosophy or another by innate traits of temperament. These sentiments later inform our political-economic position. Yes, innate; anyone with more than one child or who has cared for sibling infants with divergent characters will understand this point.

A set of distinct and irreducible principles are at the core of each political-economic theory. In a way, the theory chooses us; we're then ushered in the direction of a compatible political party. At first glance, the party seems just a label, expendable even, given its perpetual state of uncertainty from staffing changes to policy compromise. However, the party is far from dispensable; it is the proxy to a far less adaptable set of ideals. This is evidenced by the loyalty of the 'dug-in,' tolerating inconsistencies within their party's manifesto whilst swallowing countless disappointments by feckless politicians, term after term. It is not our cynicism of the other side that keeps us loyal or even the dream of a new political future. Politics dressed in rationality is cute, but don't let this sleight-of-hand swerve what's what; the bond here is spiritual.

Zoom in on the visceral interactions between left and right-wing politics; in the absence of something greater, ideologies are now the religions of the West. You may suspect that I'm flirting with determinism, and, on this rare occasion, you'd be correct, but only on the topic of political subscription. And even in this instance, change is still possible, but a spiritual change must precede it.

So, born a capitalist and still believed in the system's integrity despite getting crushed by it. And that's the right way up. It might suck but the truth cannot be compromised just because we don't like to lose. The health of our conscience and society depends on each individual's integrity; the system stands strong when its citizens ensure the metrics are valid and its politicians keep their powder dry. There's no overstating the importance of this contract; fencing our integrity violates reality itself; therefore, overall, we respect the value of truth. The prospect of a pending loss may dawn over the game, yet we will not cry penalty, at the mercy of a humiliating exam result, we will not demand a re-mark, or when life in all its triumph closes in, we will not tap out. None of this is easy and, at times, plain impossible, but civilisation hinges upon a consensus of the facts. Even as a child, I knew the truth was above us all. Back then, the truth of my life was a toss-up of pain or shame, so you can understand I respected yet was burdened by it. However, the pain was never enough for the voyeur in the school office or HR, insisting we rubber-stamp that wound by recounting the humiliating truth in exchange for sympathy that no one ordered. This is the day and the chapter we send it back.

Capitalism acutely exposes the winners and losers and the hostages, the children. And that was the hardest truth of all because all rivers seemed to lead back there. There's no overplaying the adverse effects of hardship, except maybe to those moronic altruists, and oh my, do they run aplenty. And primarily white women, why that? In striving to dignify the righteous character of minorities because we're all one homogenous blob, they cross every line. In the workplace, HR will confuse the human rights issue of equality with the business issue of competence and thereby gloss over the real effects of poverty, which most certainly impact competence. Even outside of work, we humour the altruist, recounting some friend of a friend anecdote or social study they ferreted from that one in a ten-page Google search, which suggests we can all stay honourable living on the breadline. Yet, for all that piety, they still land face-first, dignifying poverty itself. The only other probability for sporting such a witless position is they simply haven't been there.

We were not poor, but we were immigrants, of the 1980s no less, so you do the math. At the sharp end, the poorest choke on scarcity, crime and all shades of negligence and abuse. However, at the baseline is an unabating fight for healthcare, education, freedom, dignity and political representation (as a citizen, never mind the impossible odds for a refugee). Yet the worst of all deprivations is that of hope. With my own share of that pick'n'mix to contend with, I still believed in the value of hard work, speaking correctly and behaving decently. Undeniably, there were scars and, unfortunately, left unaddressed; those scars travelled like royalty straight into my future.

The system might have been compromised but not rigged. So, when my mother's car loan got rejected again, I knew it wasn't because she was African or the victim of a crooked society. Of course not. Rightly so, the look on my cynical little face denied her credit every time she made her promises to me. My mother was denied the loan because she had a chequered history of flaking out on her financial commitments, *and wot*? She was the youngest of ten children born into aristocracy. You can imagine the entitlement, but she was a long way from home, and in Great Britain, excuses don't wash. We all have destructive habits, but our future is betting on our honesty. Even if conditions appear impossible, something can always be understood or changed. I'd sooner trust myself and allow consciousness to illuminate the next step than hand the reigns to the smothering socialist. Never surrender your agency, rich or poor; it's all we'll ever have.

There is something underground racist about the diversity crusade. The world hasn't been easy on anyone, including the dark-skinned, but it's not just the world out there, is it? In my family, it was well-accepted that complexion mattered; I was the darkest, btw. Never to pass up an 'I told you so' moment; my grandmother reminded me that she had warned my young mum against her choice of a darker-skinned husband, or as she put it, following their divorce, which she'd predicted, "That's what you get for marrying a slave, they always run away." She was crazy and racist, but was she wrong? Does marital commitment challenge African men? I'm guessing we won't find research on this one. Perhaps socioeconomic or religious status has a more significant role to play over every other excuse under the sun that my dear father would have levered; God rest his pipes. Indeed, times have changed in the last two decades, and we are transitioning to a new order where African men push back against this destructive and self-fulfilling narrative, but until we're there, my money's on dead grandma.

What is missing from the narrative today, which wasn't back then, is the gift that suffering bestows. Yes, dear crusaders, the gift. Those serrated edges of life sharpened my attention, drive, courage, and resilience. It also developed my appreciation for ethics. Learning the value of integrity early doors was a blessing set up by the circumstances we're all too quick to bring to nought. If hard luck offers the education of a lifetime, then why not at least celebrate the perks? And herein lies the point: we believe in ourselves, we're making progress, and yet we're forced back there again, to the conversation of equality, by HR, of all departments. Ignored by the rest of the business, HR is still expected to clean up and bury corporate secrets with a smile; this is a tall order on any soul. Therefore, why would anyone think that a division steeped in discontent could lead the charge on questions of equality? They enjoy hearing minorities' struggles, seizing the opportunity to exert authority over anything they can, telling them there's no achievement possible without HR's interference, that even the good white guys in the corporation are corrupted by their 'privilege and unconscious bias,' that 'unconscious bias' was truly the ace in the deck. Seriously, does any part of this narrative strike you as dignifying? The diversity, equity and inclusion (DEI) agenda is not a quest for social justice but a chance for the impotent to feel powerful. However, since this authority is gained on the backs of minorities, we understand the real racist is seldom the one breaking policy but the one writing it.

Debate

Equality or Liberty?

First of all, we are not born, we do not live, and we will not die equal. Indeed, every dimension of our experience is unique. No amount of whining to the privileged or cajoling the law will bring back Santa.

It's a hard pill to swallow, but you only need to scan the US Olympic team to accept a near-zero deviation in the ethnic origin of the players of each sport. Notwithstanding the anomalies, the teams are as homogenous as farmed bass. The table tennis team? Asian. The basketball team? Black. Water polo? White frat boys with a quiff. Oh, and the 100m team? Let's move on. Why is the correlation of race or culture with aptitude acceptable in some enterprises but not others?

Alternatively, we could saddle up with the postmodernists and blame the oppressive patriarchy, which *apparently* frames our interests, character, genetics, history, you name it. They'll have us believe the whole gambit is the product of good marketing or the kind of power plays that school Machiavelli. Suppose either one of those ideas is true: inequality caused by genetic or cultural privilege benefits a few of us or a postmodernist matrix that nails us all. By both accounts, we're still unequal and demanding preferential treatment for some groups only keeps us from the solution. If we could freely celebrate the strengths of our culture and gender - honouring the differences between the feminine and masculine energies is one hope of mine - then perhaps that would make way for sober reflection on our cultural and gender-based weaknesses. Moving forward will require radical honesty and self-reflection to assess how we have arrived at this point of discontent as individuals and as a culture.

At the heels of the French Revolution, aristocrat and politician Alexis de Tocqueville penned his observations of American society and its transitioning political systems. He spotted the landmines within democratic systems and foresaw the perils of obsessive social correction. He concluded that only liberty could provide the most sustainable form of equality. God, how I wish we heeded his wisdom. In less fortunate news, theories on equity caught fire. American philosopher John Rawls had a significant influence on 20th-century political discourse. Those views took Social Contract Theory to a new level, catalysing us into the political story of the present day. Understandably, Rawls was ridden with guilt; as a child, two of his younger brothers contracted fatal illnesses from him and died just one year apart. He later became disillusioned by his time in the military, further testing his faith. The guilt plays out in his writings, which rearrange the political focus from equality to equity. Rawls' overly prescriptive approach to social justice harkens back to that guilt. Thank God there were men like Rawls, men of empathy. But empathy is a drug, just like the rest. Guilt and God are significant in this context because the DEI mission appeals to the faithless, to hard-boiled sceptics of the establishment, to the neurosis of bureaucratic and corporate reformers, to the shame of the *haves* and the vengeance of the *have-nots*. And guess what? We're still unequal.

Bigger Fish

The hunters of utopia need not lose another night's sleep over the crusade for equality. The last iteration of generative AI is already making good on labour market headwinds. Within a string of updates, AI will sweep in to rinse through the final traces of middle management and maybe spare enough bytes to convert our kids and make a pass at our husbands.

Speaking of shameless pseudo-intelligence, this summer, I read a McKinsey article on generative AI; the author seemed quite taken by the industry's prospects in its next wave, estimating that a good run in the coming decades could generate $2-4 trillion of growth. Those consulting bandits truly understand the art of the shakedown. You know you're the best of the worst when you're able to publish insights on social equity and diversity, then, after lunch, sketch the most effective OxyContin distribution strategies. Of course, they are not the only ones. And whilst they may have settled for their pharma sins, what of the sin of duplicity? Who really gives a hoot about DEI, and how does any of this wash?

Discrimination may exist, but we have bigger fish. When AI is through with this strait of the economy, and the effects cascade throughout society, we'll realise those shit jobs were all that guarded that homeless guy's conscience. The streets in the City of London wouldn't be the same again; his interruptions may have once inconvenienced my lunch, but now he'll save the red tape and knock me out cold in front of my colleagues. You see, in London's financial district, we have homeless beggars who, by day, are fully compos mentis, not swaying in some San Fran-style stupor. Therefore, the once cordial eye-to-eye between the *haves* and the *have-nots* is increasingly precarious in these economic times.

Fellow *Sapiens*, Yuval's probably right; it's better to have a shit job than none at all. This dark dystopia will have us romanticising the past centuries of exploitation; when at least, our value to the economy was still a topic of discussion. In search of freedom and equality, the Israelites of *The Exodus* marched into the desert, where they languished for decades, lost and forgotten. In losing their purpose, their self-worth was reduced to less than when slaves; this had them reminiscing and yearning a return to the banks of the Nile. Debating our professional value through the free market or the unions beats proving our existence altogether.

XX

Women run the world. Since the dawn of reproduction, females have pulled the strings of civilisation. Female mating patterns aggregate and normalise to define the culture's sexual ideal of character, physique, and status. One might assume it is the same in reverse, but it is not. If we pop the hood, we'll understand the game was rigged against men aeons before that stony look she shot at the bar.

Mitochondria are the organelles responsible for the spark that gives us life. Without this process, we couldn't convert fuel to energy; development at the cellular level would degenerate entirely. In other words, no life. Back when this promising gent was a sprightly sperm, his success was contingent upon the judgy egg in waiting. In 2020, researchers at Stockholm and Manchester Universities discovered that strength isn't the only decider of the winning sperm. The egg sends a chemical signal, her siren call, stimulating only a selection from the surviving sperm to up their efficiency to the finish line. Should he succeed in fertilising the egg, he'd soon discover an institutional discrimination that neither he nor his future male lineage could escape.

You see, both males and females have mitochondria living in every cell. Mitochondria have their own DNA (mtDNA); however, theirs is sourced exclusively from the mother. Natural selection grossly biases female fitness, not just us but all living species (with few exceptions). This bias is expressed in the optimisation process of the female's mtDNA; for her, pathogenic mutations are eliminated, and beneficial mutations are retained. Nature, however, pays no mind to the adverse effects these female-centred modifications may have on male mtDNA. As mutations harmful to males are ignored, the mutant load accumulates over generations. This genetic catch leaves males increasingly more vulnerable to lower fertility levels, disease and an earlier grave, as we've all come to jest. Compensatory moves within the nuclear genome serve the male's defence, but this clapback is no comparison to the offensive. Finally, nature's prudence covers both ends of this transaction; the now healthier, optimised mtDNA is passed down exclusively to females, ensuring no socialism creeps in to level out this injustice.

Back to female rule, for those who enjoy cartoons, it may appear that males throughout history dominated the governance of civilisations. I advise those who eat this up to acquaint themselves with some light anthropology before pissing on state or corporate policy. Let's clear this up now. Women decide if to mate, who to mate, and when to mate. Antagonised by his biology and female rejection, finally, when he dreams of a better future, at least for his descendants, he is brutally reminded that she and she alone decides if his unborn child punches in. Ladies, the world we view as unfair is of our making; we propagated the male ideal that toxic feminists love to hate. And that, my sorority sisters, is the biological and societal, inescapable matriarchy.

Poverty: Symptom or the Cause?

In a discussion with Jordan Peterson, British comedian Russell Brand once described a poignant experience he encountered as an aspiring celebrity. The story was of a time when Brand offered to share his home with a homeless man. Whilst appreciated by the troubled soul, Brand's generosity was eventually cut short by the homeless man voluntarily returning to his precarious circumstances.

Poverty is far more complex than we would like to admit. Please resist the urge to misinterpret this sentiment as a justification for society's resignation to this problem. One of the most challenging exercises in data analysis is proving direct causation over correlation. I'm convinced chronic adult hardship in the developed world is a symptom of a more fundamental issue than rising unemployment levels, something closer to mental illness. Not just theirs but ours too, as we refuse to think more deeply and productively about uncomfortable social troubles.

It breaks my heart to see someone unsheltered, to know that, at that moment, the person does not have a single friend or relative they could or would want to call. They become the living dead. We all suffer, but they must suffer all day, all night, and publicly without dignity. Discrimination exists, but I do not believe it is the driving force that creates poverty. Political-economic systems, culture, character, addiction, relationships, and crime could accelerate an individual's downturn. However, at the epicentre of this story is its most powerful influence, the individual who pilots it all. 19-20th-century Swiss psychoanalyst Carl Jung expressed his concept of the psyche in *The Archetypes and the Collective Unconscious*, this reminds us that darkness within the individual is immeasurably more potent than any external force, "A man who is possessed by his shadow is always standing in his own light and falling into his own traps...living below his own level." The privileges of the first percentile needn't smear the equality debate because clearing their bank accounts will not move the needle on the quality of our existence. A reset of the material will be a fleeting win, and on the morning after, we'll soon understand the forces governing prosperity run deeper than we wish to look. The *haves* believe in their value and their power. Could it be that my poverty has nothing to do with the riches of another?

The nature and complexity of poverty is such that it deserves its own chapter, that's for next time. However, poverty has been relevant to this chapter because the DEI mission has labelled it both a cause and symptom of discrimination; yet, poverty is a symptom of a mental affliction, which is a much bigger problem. For now, let us be of the same mind on the limits of reason: production of wealth may elevate the comforts of the rich, and redistribution of wealth may blunt the suffering of the poor, but the cause of poverty lives on. Private jets and clean needles are no match for a broken soul.

Getting Real; It's All Your Fault

When I encounter injustice, my first impulse is to question how I invited this event to my door. Let's at least be honest about the root cause of human-inflicted suffering. Much of it we can trace back to our regrettable judgement, and some we're burdened with by association. We, individuals, pay for the sins of our culture, but we also benefit from the good of our culture.

Is it wrong, and I do not mean discriminatory, but wrong, that a CV sporting an address of a crime hotspot is declined? Let's unpack precisely what is being rejected. Growing up exposed to that environment will have impacted the applicant's mental state, delivering some positive features such as resilience and resourcefulness, which should prove valuable in a competitive work environment. Then, there are habits that, perhaps, are not so transferable. Even if I were the best kid on the block who avoided trouble, there's no telling what I witnessed or became accustomed to. No doubt, this trauma is fated to express itself in the future, including in the workplace. So, whose fault is this? The applicant who has already been through the wringer and is desperately trying to build a new life? The interviewer being advised that serving a rejection is discriminatory, and is forced to deny his trusted instincts? What about the culture, from the side that blames the privileged winners to the B-side that tells me and other minorities we're destined to lose? What's their share in all of this?

It doesn't matter. Know why? Because it's still on me. Play this out: if the company is genuinely corrupt and discriminates on non-profit yielding markers, capitalism will eat them alive. And if they don't fold, then their practices will become common knowledge - courtesy of the Age of Information. I love it that consumers have realised they have a seat at the table, perhaps the most powerful seat. The fair-trade movement began in the 1940s through the efforts of religious charities and NGOs raising awareness of the inhumane conditions experienced by developing world workers. But we all know the limits of our attention span regarding the sympathy vote. Sympathy matters, but it's not nearly as effective as when combined with the urge to punish those in power. This cocktail shapeshifts listed companies to their knees. And the best part of a boycott is it needn't involve a single politician. That's the beauty of the free market. Therefore, if the company is rotten, I apply elsewhere because Mother Nature is far more exacting than any letter of complaint.

Bad actors are all over the shop; still, I must ensure I'm not one of them. First stop, elocution; I've no idea how English-speaking Americans communicate with some of their fellow citizens who refuse to learn the official language and have somehow legitimised ghetto-speak. Learn the god-damn language properly, find a way, YouTube it, whatever. Next, I'll have to choose my people, talk like them, eat their food, smell like them (evolutionary biologists can't drop that one), get their jokes, dress even better than them, and ignore the echoes of sour grapes from my native culture trying to drag me back; I'm no 'Uncle Tom.' This is a natural law that applies to everyone, not just minorities: the man who requests a pay rise with zero conviction, the mum who bores her team recounting her children's routine, or the polygender who is wondering why their colleagues seem pensive. We must adapt to the game and master it long before we can change it. When it comes to progress, financial or otherwise, everything is relational, so it's either our past or our future, and in the event we prefer to ignore this reality, our actions will choose for us.

Gender

The LGBTQ2+etc group of individuals, hereafter referred to as non-hetero, is the minority group that suffers most significantly in almost all societies. Without delving into the unknowable, i.e., the validity of each letter on the gender spectrum or, indeed, the spectrum itself, let us focus on the effects of this movement. I hate to join the pissing contest on who has had it worst, but we must hold ourselves accountable for the shitty things we've said, done, seen, or ignored. Throughout history, non-heteros have been judged, insulted, assaulted, and alienated at work, home, and abroad. Non-heteros worldwide still face inhumane treatment inflicted by a diverse range of homophobes, and it barely makes the village news. Much of this has occurred without familial or therapeutic support; this is a stain on our conscience.

This shame has been addressed in a counterproductive way. Gender identification is no longer considered a mental health issue but a political one. There's an interesting correlation between this topic and racism. The management levels of the public and private sectors have absconded from this debate. I understand the anxiety stemming from legal concerns and reputational injury. But a fear of pronoun misuse or perceived bigotry is no reason to fold. Indeed, that surrender has occurred across Western democracies and is why we're now subordinate to that HR person who has long been dreaming of this day, and here it is. She can now project her impotence straight onto executives too spooked to do what they're paid to: lead. And here we are, at the back end of the mother of all corporate landgrabs.

There is more to this catastrophe than getting schooled by the diversity mascot. In female-only sports, biological males turn up to collect, not compete for, but collect gold medals. And at the shittier end of this circus, they show up to pulverise female MMA champions. My first child was born in a highly reputed London hospital, and there I was handed a pamphlet that referred to me as a 'pregnant person.' That nonsense was a decade ago. Imagine that. Sexualising school kids through grotesquely detailed sex education in the primary years and chasing that with a rotating ceremony to present the next new gender doesn't feel like a march on inclusivity. Children need to feel grounded in their most sensitive development years; sporadically, pulling the rug on their identity is disorienting and cruel.

Closing Tavistock, the child gender identity clinic in the UK, is a step in the right direction. US hospitals have shown an incline in paediatric reassignment services delivered; in addition, the community health centres, which are more prevalent (1400 and counting), are far more driven within local communities. Apparently, 'non-profit' federally funded and indemnified health centres have Washington's blessing to push child gender transitioning advisory services. So, Uncle Sam cuts them a check to deliver their services and another to pay insurance claims for practices insurers would never underwrite. This is not just some innocuous way to boost tax-free surpluses (profits); cooking the books in the name of health is pretty low, and then there's leveraging the insecurities of American teens to pump receipts. Wow.

Doctors are penned between action and inaction; malpractice lawsuits are coming in left and right, a Discrimination charge for rejecting reassignment surgery and Gross Negligence for performing it. This predicament is ridiculous, but at least it will compel the general public to engage in this debate; our children's rights and future are at stake. This should matter.

Why didn't we choose one new pronoun encompassing all non-conventional sexual interests? Keep it simple because we don't need to know how you like your eggs in the morning; it's none of our business. We didn't create a fixed non-hetero acronym because we had no idea this story was immortal. The gender discussion needn't feature in the public arena. Where necessary, the use of such information may be reserved for official purposes. Beyond this, sex is biology, and the rest is private; that way, no one's getting offended or sued. Last question: Why didn't we create a separate category within sports championships to allow trans people to compete against one another? Or at least instate (or improve) a strength class system that scrutinises the players' physique. And lastly, please let children be children.

Mums

A word for maternity returners. You should hire them, not because they deserve it, but because you do. A mother has all the smarts of the rest but an efficiency rate that surpasses her peers by orders of magnitude.

By her third pregnancy, a few of us may have questioned whether she was *on the take*. Yes, she's taken time out of the industry, of life itself, to raise children, as our mothers did for us, but she's also the only hope the economy has. How else do we propose to rebalance those ageing demographics? Darwinian pressures aside, whilst *on the take*, she was learning to cut out excuses, inspire, protect, and deliver every day to the sound of loud, unappreciative cries or, if lucky, to silence. She returns with greater resolve and everything to prove. You can bet she'll complete that project first and floor your expectations. Best part is, she probably did it the slowest way imaginable when accounting for IT losses.

Tyranny

Tocqueville asserted that tyranny could manifest in any number of forms, most notably because of the heedless devolution of power to a large majority or, paradoxically, as we witness today, to a multitude of minority interests and groups. This one we can nip in the bud real quick. To varying degrees, all of us are corruptible, primarily by open self-interest, but also in a more closeted virtuous form, such as the DEI mission. Corporations have been quick to appoint underqualified minorities into high-profile positions to the detriment of all parties. These actions not only embarrass the appointee, all exposed and out of their depth, the staff who were already disillusioned with the so-called meritocracy, but worst of all, this shames the corporation.

Hats off to the Harvard Business Review for signing off on the 2019 article, which pointed out that 88% of the S&P500 companies are owned by a crowd of three: BlackRock, Vanguard and State Street. And all it took for corporations on both sides of the Atlantic to twerk to the tune of ESG was for this rat pack to drive this newly minted product, yes, product, to the top of boardroom agendas. In its acceptance of the ESG mandate and metrics, the corporation all but admitted that before the World Economic Forum's little hissy fit, it was a discriminatory employer. Corporations sold the farm for a choice of two titles: puppet or fraud.

Despite the repugnant monopoly over capital markets, on the shop floor, the villain is rarely the kingpin. Heterosexual minorities and white diversity champions have committed most of the discriminatory behaviour I have encountered in business. Asians, especially those still close with their parents, ignored me altogether; fine by me, at least it's honest and impersonal. Asians rarely troubled me except on the rare occasion they would find themselves in a senior position, in which case they'd gleefully swipe the ladder, but this was rare because often their application for a management promotion was rejected, as they struggled to shift gears from teacher's pet to magnanimous leader. Then there were the Blacks, punch drunk on retribution (or DEI goals), who hated me for pulling rank. White Westerners who had not embroiled themselves cradle to grave in the DEI cult were most open to my rise.

Respect is Earned, not Redistributed

There is no greater oppression than one that so powerfully subverts our sovereignty. And yet, in the name of equity, this oppressor has subdued the most prominent institutions that have existed to civilise our Western societies. I wonder where it ends as we watch yet another scientist take 'the knee' in support of the reigning Left. This manifests in many ways: in the burial of research identifying inconvenient differences between ethnicities or endorsing a perversion of the facts as with biological sex.

Indeed, objective reality is back on the table. What sorcery. In broad daylight, the game is now fully decked with unearned university admissions and corporate promotions, unjust prison clemency, and a reparations process blighted by bureaucrats bidding for their share in a slave buyback scheme. That's the most egregious part: this bag of goodies is exchanged for our souls, slaves again. Manifesting Alt-Right dreams through a Leftist movement, now that's one hell of a racket. Only socialism, regrettably with our blessing, could violate our dignity so profoundly. FYI, this is actual discrimination. It is high time we recover our dignity, no sooner our divinity. Socialist and postmodernist power, save your pity party. You're not my keeper, and I am not your project, but you know this, don't you? You see the fortune within the underprivileged: ambitious, strong and unentitled. The only way to hold us back is to remind us we were once yours. Shit, you almost had us. But the world is waking up.

Conclusion: Life vs. Utopia

Perception of reality is quite a curious case. Often, I've questioned if the world's issues are uncomplicated to resolve as the present culture portrays. And by that token, all that stands between here and utopia is merely a series of witch-hunts, petitions and protests. As if. It brings me great relief that we are not the subjects of a facile world in which the source of our pain could always be blamed upon someone or some group. If reality were that simple, we would have surrendered the best parts of life: sovereignty, love and faith. Let's give that a test run.

The first casualty of postmodernist rule is the individual's sovereignty. You are a product of your circumstances; thus, you are neither the cause nor the solution to your suffering. Moreover, the cause of your suffering is most certainly a fellow human being, group or the socially constructed system. Therefore, you needn't bother yourself with dreams of self-improvement since you're no match for the governing forces oppressing you. Indeed, you exist exclusively within the context of the collective, without which you would not survive.

What is love? Society may be driven by compassion for the weak. However, compassion is a narcotic with just a flicker of a half-life, and it's only the opening act to the star of the show that is here to stay: resentment. Soon, we'll all feel inclined to compete for sympathy in a race to the bottom of our own self-respect. Sympathy is the axe the postmodernist uses to gain power. Indeed, sympathy is used to assault our traditions and values in the name of honouring black criminals and vilifying police for daring to defend themselves or protect us. Political crusades of compassion are not love. Isn't love based on truth? Whatever love is it is not the tacky high bought with affirmative action.

Life now unfolds under the exacting rule of zero-sum economics, so life becomes predictable. Of course, every injustice must be balanced; therefore, faith has no function as restitution can and will be delivered through legal or political means. Faith has no function because you now count out your days in a Western autocracy. That's enough of that nightmare.

Faith buffers us from the hell of the postmodernist paradise. Make no mistake: history has shown injustice and equality to be in constant surplus and deficit, nevertheless, the markers are tracking in the right direction. The Organisation for Economic Co-operation and Development (OECD) is one of several organisations to compile holistic metadata on human development. Across the last two centuries, the OECD found that global GDP has risen 70 times, and the remaining metrics on well-being covering a range of personal and political conditions have improved substantially for most countries. Admittedly, data availability of the geographies and time intervals analysed wasn't always consistent, but it's the best we have. It is also worth underlining Western values were used to assess human development. Nevertheless, we can settle objectively that total economic production, human rights, and overall comfort levels have improved significantly. So that's good, *right*?

Despite clear evidence of continued gains and injustice on its descent, contentment for the postmodernist glides in a day late and a dollar short. It's never enough, is it? There's nothing to be proud of or to celebrate; pessimism is the only constant. Reason has starved this soul, no longer enchanted by the beauty, love or the promise of something so much more.

Optimism, without faith in a higher power, is near impossible. Faith invites us to trust in a benevolent universe, seeking equilibrium; the invisible hand is not only a metaphor for the free market. In holding faith, we can trust that each divine being lives in his genius and with his suffering intimately in ways the rest of us will never know.

Last year, sitting in traffic, shooting the breeze with my eldest daughter, I asked her what miracle she would wish for, and she responded,

"Nothing, Mum, wishes are for those who don't believe."

Thank You

I'm truly humbled that we shared this moment. My intention was to discuss a selection of ideas pertinent to our time; I was never religious, so I did not expect to fall absolutely in love with God as I did.

Until we meet again.

DEDICATION

With deep gratitude to my parents for your beautiful contribution to humanity. Political dissidents under an African dictator who was burning up Christians. You summoned the will to sacrifice everything we had or could have had to stand up to tyranny in the name of true democracy. An atheist and a Muslim at the front line of politics defending the freedom of Christians under siege.

Pure love.

And to my school English teachers, who saw the light in a refugee; because of you, I'm here.

Mrs Winterburn, Mrs Brandt, and Mrs Sommers.

Printed in Poland
by Amazon Fulfillment
Poland Sp. z o.o., Wrocław
01 November 2023

fe7f8575-2b7e-4919-b655-c5e44ed84eb1R01